One
April
Morning

One April Morning

Children Remember the Oklahoma City Bombing

by Nancy Lamb
and Children of Oklahoma City
illustrated by Floyd Cooper

Lothrop, Lee & Shepard Books
New York

*T*o the living in honor of those who died

*S*ome tragedies crush spirits. Other tragedies transform them. When the bomb exploded, the heart of Oklahoma was broken. Miraculously, when that heart mended, it had grown bigger.

However, it wasn't only Oklahomans who rallied to the sides of those whose lives had been damaged and destroyed by the bomb. It was men and women and children throughout the world.

And so it is to all those people—the ones who gave their time and comfort and caring to the recovery effort, the ones who gave new meaning to generosity of spirit—that we dedicate this book.

—N. L. and F. C.

Text copyright © 1996 by Nancy Lamb
Illustrations copyright © 1996 by Floyd Cooper
All rights reserved. No part of this book may be reproduced or utilized in any form or by any means,
electronic or mechanical, including photocopying and recording, or by any information storage and retrieval system,
without permission in writing from the Publisher. Inquiries should be addressed to
Lothrop, Lee & Shepard Books, a division of William Morrow & Company, Inc.,
1350 Avenue of the Americas, New York, New York 10019.
Printed in the United States of America
First Edition   1 2 3 4 5 6 7 8 9 10
Library of Congress Cataloging in Publication Data
Lamb, Nancy. One April morning: children remember the Oklahoma City bombing /
by Nancy Lamb and children of Oklahoma City; illustrated by Floyd Cooper.
p.   cm.   Summary: Conversations with children from the Oklahoma City area about their feelings
at the time of the bombing of the Federal Building and afterwards.
ISBN 0-688-14666-X. — ISBN 0-688-14724-0 (lib.bdg.)
1. Oklahoma City Federal Building Bombing, Oklahoma City, Okla.,1995—Juvenile literature.
2. Children—Oklahoma—Oklahoma City—Psychology—Juvenile literature. 3. Post-traumatic stress disorder in children—Oklahoma—Oklahoma City—Juvenile literature.[1. Oklahoma City Federal Building Bombing, Oklahoma City, Okla.,1995. 2. Psychic trauma.]
I. Cooper, Floyd, ill. II. Title. HV6432.L35 1996 976.6'38—dc20 95-39210 CIP AC

A NOTE FROM THE AUTHOR

I was visiting friends and family in Oklahoma City when the bomb exploded. Two months later, I returned to my home town to talk with children about the disaster that had so sadly disrupted their lives. Those children directly involved in the blast—whether by injury or loss of a parent or sibling—were, of course, still too fragile to participate in the writing of a book such as this. But others who were deeply affected by the bombing were eager to share their thoughts and feelings with me and with the children who will read this book. Without exception, the children I met welcomed me with warmth and talked to me with openness, honesty, and sincerity.

In the course of my interviews, I traveled from Yukon to Martin Luther King Boulevard, from Hefner Road to Midwest City to S.E. 92nd, talking to kids whose ages ranged from three to fourteen. Geographically and ethnically separated, the children were bound by tragedy and loss. In spite of this—or perhaps because of it—they demonstrated a wisdom beyond their years as they told me about feelings, taught me about healing, and showed me a path to acceptance. For all of this, I am immensely grateful.

Nancy Lamb
September 1995

A LETTER TO PARENTS AND TEACHERS

The purpose of this book is to help children cope with the emotional confusion that follows in the wake of trauma and loss. Hearing the fearful and honest voices of children who have walked this painful path before them can make other children feel more comfortable about expressing their own feelings and concerns with those who love them most.

Children who have experienced trauma will often show us their stress rather than discuss their feelings. For instance, instead of talking about the incident, some children might undergo changes in sleeping and eating patterns. Others might regress in toilet habits or have difficulties in separating from their parents. These normal responses to trauma are outward manifestations of unexpressed feelings and usually run their course after a few months. (Prolonged symptoms can be indications that the child might need some counseling to help him or her overcome the stress of the situation.)

This book offers adults a way into those scary places where children hide in order to protect themselves and those they love. Instead of exposing their vulnerability and pain, children often retreat into silence, sadly unable to find the words they need to express themselves. It is in the isolation of unexpressed emotions that the devastation is felt most deeply, because children feel there is no one with whom to share their feelings, their fears, and their questions.

Reading this book with your children provides a way for you to acknowledge their trauma safely while being available to them if they want to explore the feelings surrounding their pain and fear. Initially, the process of revealing feelings might be scary. But once the door to expression is open, the healing can finally begin.

Anne Early, L.C.S.W., A.C.S.W.

THE JOURNEY OF HEALING

On the day that I was asked to help the families of those killed in the bombing, I did not know what to expect. I only knew it would be difficult. The death of one person is tragic enough. This was *169 people*, and it was not only death and loss that people had to confront, it was trauma and shock, innocence and helplessness, fear and rage. For me, reaching out to the families was a small effort to help. For those suffering, the experience was a soul-shattering loss.

Yet we know that people survive life-transforming traumas. If they are successful in the process we call grieving, they go forward—never the same, but deeper, possibly richer in heart, with the lost ones forever part of themselves.

Out of the horrible events of April 19th, an outpouring of help and caring, comfort and love came from throughout the nation and around the world. All who reached out had to first let themselves feel the pain of the people in Oklahoma City. Each act of caring became part of that person's grieving and healing.

This book is an account of and an act of healing, one that comes from Nancy Lamb and the children she talked with. Their emotional journey reflects many aspects of everyone's journey through the daunting process of recovering from trauma. Whether that trauma is caused by a death, an accident, abuse, a fire or flood, an earthquake, a war, a suicide or bomb, the feelings we must face are similar: shock, denial, helplessness, numbness, the gradual pain of awareness, sorrow, anger, guilt, depression, fear turning to fury, the pain of more remembering, the appreciation of what is lost and what is left, love, hope, the slowly developing will to mend, and finally the gradual integration of this process into a transformed life with forever different love and joy. Strength can be gained from this personal healing journey. If you have suffered, I believe this book can help your journey or the journey of a child you love.

Mary Ann Coates, L.C.S.W., B.C.D.

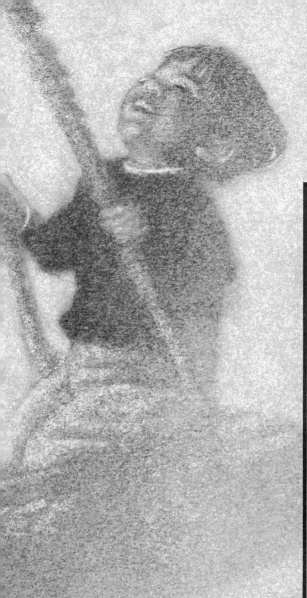

BEFORE

April 19, 1995, seemed like a regular Wednesday in Oklahoma. Grown-ups were at work, children were in school, and the world felt perfectly normal. Suddenly, at 9:02 in the morning, a car bomb exploded in front of the Alfred P. Murrah Federal Building in Oklahoma City.

When the smoke cleared, the north side of the building looked like a giant had stomped his foot on it in a fit of rage, squashing steel, concrete, and marble into a pile of sorrow-filled rubble.

- more than 500 people were wounded in the explosion
- 169 people were killed
- 19 children died and more than 100 children lost one or both parents in the bombing

The shock of the explosion stunned the nation. Nobody ever thought that the worst terrorist bombing in the history of the United States could happen in such a peaceful place as Oklahoma City.

First came a bumping rumble.
Then came a rolling roar.
The ground jiggled like Jell-O and
a savage blast cracked the quiet morning calm.
Fingers of fire reached high in the sky,
and broken glass, blown by the bomb,
sprayed danger in every direction.

"Windows in my school exploded," said Aimee Ann.
"I thought it was thunder," said Todd.
"It was a big bump," said Tiara.
"Boom!" said Nori. "It went BOOM!"
"All the lights went out and there was a big, big explosion,"
said Christina.
"There was fire everywhere," said Ryan.

"I was scared," said Julie.

For miles all around,
everyone felt the force of the bomb.
Sidewalks shimmied and buildings shook.
Concrete broke and windows shattered
as bitter clouds of smoke fouled the air,
and everywhere across the city, hearts trembled.

"My daddy fell out of his chair," said Ryan.
"We could see black smoke from the window,"
said Aimee Ann.
"Everything blew everywhere," said Stephanie.
"Stuff fell from the ceiling and all the pictures cracked,"
said Todd.
"All of a sudden we heard this big boom," said Cicely.
"The trees bent over and the doors flew open."

"It was scary," said Bailey.

"It was terrifying," said Aimee Ann.
"Everybody was screaming."

Fire fighters and police officers, priests and parents,
doctors and nurses, friends and strangers,
rushed to the scene of the blast.
Wails of sirens drowned out cries for help
as injured people, dazed and bleeding,
wandered from the bombed-out buildings.
Others, less fortunate, were trapped inside.
At hospitals all over the city, emergency teams assembled
to await the arrival of the wounded.

"My mommy was at the hospital," said Gracie.
"She was looking out for all the people."
"My daddy is a doctor. He went to his hospital," said Rachel.
"He waited and waited for someone he could help.
But nobody came because most of the people were dead."
"There were parents walking around outside the building
with pictures of their kids, asking if anybody had seen them,"
said Brad.

"I was scared," said Melissa, "because my mom was downtown."
"I was scared," said Brendon. "My guts were scared
and I was trying to hide somewhere."

Stronger than a hurricane wind,
louder than crashing thunder,
the helter-skelter bomb blast even blew away
the clothes that people wore.

"My daddy got a two-year-old baby out of the ambulance,"
said Addi. "It only had socks on."

"I felt mad and sorry," said Rachel.
"I didn't know how I felt," said Erika.

In homes and hospitals,
in schools and stores,
everybody cried.
Nurses and doctors cried.
Rescue workers and fire fighters cried.

*"At night my mom was crying because she had to
see all those people with no legs and arms,"
said Dillon.*

"All the kids were crying," said Stephanie.
"I cried because all those people died," said Addi.
"My mama got tears in her eyes," said Tiara.
"My mommy was crying," said Julie.
*"I saw my parents crying, and I knew it was bad,"
said Aimee Ann.*
"I never saw a man cry before," said Nori.

*"The first night it rained,
it seemed like God was crying, too,"
said Emili.*

Wrapped in sadness, buried in grief,
families and friends waited for news
of their loved ones.
Hundreds of people searched for survivors.
Thousands of people cared for the living.
Millions of people mourned for the dead.

"People lost their babies and nieces and nephews.
They lost grandchildren and daughters and mothers,"
said Emili.
"My assistant Girl Scout Leader died," said Cicely.
"My friend's father had a piece of glass
stuck in the back of his head," said Christina.
"My friend's mom got killed," said Joshua.

"I felt mad and angry," said Jenna.

"God doesn't like people destroying His world,"
said Addi.

Caught between disbelief and horror,
the world watched and wept
as flags flew at half-mast,
heads hung in sadness,
and hearts sang a sorrowful song.

"I had trouble sleeping," said Abby.
"I had nightmares," said Bonny.
"I started to sleepwalk," said Todd.
"My brother started sleeping on the bottom bunk,"
said Rachel.
"I couldn't sleep," said Virginia.
"I tried sleeping on the floor,
and finally fell asleep under my bed."
"I had the scaredest dream in the house,"
said Brendon.

"When we'd hear a loud noise that wasn't normal,"
said Courtney, "we were always wondering
what it was and what could happen."

"It all felt like a bad dream," said Emili.

Along with the buildings,
along with the lives of innocent people
and the hopes and dreams of survivors,
the explosion also destroyed
the sense of security
the children had always lived with.

"Anything can happen to anyone, anytime, anywhere," said Emili.

"There could be a bomb right here," said Abby. "At my school, at my house, even in my car."

"You can't really control what happens," said Cicely.

Numb with shock and pain,
Oklahomans sat in front of their televisions
and watched fire fighters struggle
with the overwhelming task of searching for survivors.
Day after windy day,
night after freezing night,
in cold and stormy weather,
workers dug through the rubble,
their hearts as tattered as their gloves.
Hope and fear followed the rescue dogs
into the bombed-out building
as they searched for the living
and discovered the dead.

"Those rescue workers were real heroes," said Alecia.

*"I know one guy," said Brad, "who pulled a whole bunch of people out.
I was worried that there would be another bomb while he was down there."*

*"It was brave of them to go in there," said Rachel.
"What if the floor caved in and then the ceiling?"*

Images of the explosion
filled television screens across the land.
Stories of grieving parents and wounded children
shared time with tales of a community working together.

*"I felt guilty that I was at home watching TV and there might
still be people alive in there," said Brad.
"The teachers at school, they wanted us to put it behind us
and concentrate on our work," said Courtney. "But you can't,
because it's the only thing that's really on your mind."
"It's hard not to think about it," said Emili.*

"Sometimes you can be mad and sad at the same time," said Virginia.

"I didn't know what to feel, or what to believe," said Cicely.

Anxious and confused, people looked around and thought,
"There must be something I can do."

Support began with a trickle and turned into a flood.
Throughout Oklahoma, thousands of people
stood in line for hours to give blood.
In the city, thousands more carried socks
and food and warm clothes to the workers.
They brought booties and biscuits for the search-and-rescue dogs.
They donated money and parkas and raincoats.
They sent blankets and flowers, boots and gloves,
candy and towels and teddy bears.
And when the rescue workers came off duty
after digging in the bombed-out building for twelve hours,
they were met by counselors
who helped them cope with their sadness
and treated to massages that rubbed away their aches and pains.

I donated my allowance for a month," said Macey.
"We made six sausages and thirty banana breads," said Deana.
"And our school raised fourteen hundred dollars.
Kids just kept donating their lunch money."
"At school we sold popcorn in third grade and donated sixty dollars,"
said Bailey.
"I gave two dollars and so did my sisters," said Addi.

Churches opened their doors to anyone in need of help.
Therapists volunteered their time to talk to frightened people,
television stations raised money to pay for hospital bills of the wounded,
and restaurants donated food to feed the volunteers.
Each night when the rescue workers went to bed,
a thank-you letter from a child was lying on each pillow.

"Everybody came together. Everybody helped each other," said Abby.
"I was real proud."

"The people in Oklahoma City were like a rope," said Chad.
"The middle of the rope was burned, but the strands held together."

Like a monster in the closet
who creeps out of the midnight dark,
anger with the people who set off the bomb
sparked unanswered questions and confusing thoughts
in the minds of all the children.
How could you do this? they asked.
How could you take everything away
from people who did you no harm?
Why did you do this?

"Why?" asked Cicely. "You hurt my friends' feelings, you hurt me,
and you hurt my family. Don't you feel anything?"

"Those people caused a lot of sadness," said Ramsey.
"I think those people should be ashamed of themselves," said Ashley.
"That man who did this made the devil look good," said Brendon.
"He made the devil cry down there. The devil said, 'Why do you insult me?
I was supposed to be the evilest one. Now you make me look bad.'"

"Why couldn't you use words instead of bombs?" said Cicely.
"Why do you have to get rid of all those innocent people, too?"

"Everybody gets mad at the government," said Courtney.
"But that's no reason to go bomb a building."

"Why did God let this happen?" asked Josh.

The children thought a lot about the bad men.
Struggling with their feelings,
they wondered what should be done
with someone who creates such deliberate evil.

"I think he should be in jail for all his life," said William.
"I think he should be put to death," said Jack.
"But before that, the people who lost loved ones
should come by and meet in front of him."
"The man who did this should go through a long
and sorrowful death," said Stephanie.
"I think he should get electrocuted in the chair," said Tiara.

"I think we should give him a fair trial first," said Dillon.

"I think we should put him in jail and let him stay with the monsters,"
said Gracie. "Or we should put him in a tank and let the sharks eat him."
"These people can ask God to forgive them," said Argelia.
"But it's not just saying sorry with words. It has to come from the heart."
"I can't forgive them," said Michael,
"because I don't understand how to forgive them."

I don't think we as a human race have
any right to kill anybody else," said Courtney.

"I don't think we should execute the people who did
this," said Melissa, "because if we kill them, that
makes us killers, too."

"There's nothing you could ever do to the people
who exploded the bomb that would be justice to
them," said Emili. "They can't be in the place of the
mothers who lost their children and feel the pain that
they feel. And they can't feel the pain of the lady that
was trapped under concrete and the rescuers left her
inside the building because of another bomb threat.
They'll never feel how frightened she was."

More than the destruction,
more than a sorrow-filled city and the death of adults,
the death of the babies upset the children most of all.

*"At school we planted a redbud tree for each child who
died," said Jamie.*
"We planted some flowers," said Connie.
*"We didn't ever think that babies would be killed like that,"
said Courtney.*
"They were the innocent ones," said Aleah.
"Those children should go to heaven," said Darbi.
"They will go to heaven," said Leticia.
*"Those babies should have had a taste of happiness
before they had to go upstairs," said Chad.*
*"I hope they're going to get all the love they need up there,"
said Cicely.*

"I know they're in a bigger and better place," said Rachel.

Overcome by sadness,
the children understood that the babies who died
would never feel another good-night kiss
or sing another song.
They'd never go swimming or hiking,
or learn how to read or ride a bike.
They'd never dance or laugh or chase a butterfly.

"The children lost the most," said Emili.
"They didn't get to grow up.
They'll never know the wonder of things."

"They'll miss the earth and the beautiful scenery,"
said Courtney.
"They'll never get to eat ice cream," said Josh.
"They'll never get to go skating or see a movie
or play hide-and-seek," said Tiara.

"They'll never get to blow the puffs off a dandelion,"
said Emili.

For weeks after the bombing,
hundreds of thousands of cards and letters and gifts
poured into Oklahoma City from across the nation
and around the world.

So many pictures and letters from children arrived,
every shopping mall in the city was decorated with them.
Teddy bears came from Oregon and Iowa,
Illinois and Pennsylvania.
Angel pins came from Colorado and Missouri and Vermont.
As a symbol of healing, a garland of one thousand origami
paper cranes was sent from a school in North Carolina.
Students from Puerto Rico visited students in Oklahoma City.
A school in Japan sent a video camera
to a school in Oklahoma.
And in California, a ten-year-old boy named Spencer
organized a snack shack at his elementary school and raised
$142.50 to help pay for the injured children's hospital bills.

"The kids from other states were wonderful to us," said Melissa.
"I got twenty-eight different letters," said Abby.
"When I answered the letters," said Alecia,
"I thanked them for writing and caring."

"If we didn't have the help from everybody else," said Courtney,
"it would have been a lot harder to pull together."

As the children started to understand
that they could make the world better
by changing their own lives,
they realized that expressing their feelings
helped them cope with their fears.

"When you're scared, what do you want to do?" said Dillon.
"You want to be with people you love…to be with friends
and parents and relatives because they can comfort you."
"Mothers and fathers should listen to their kids," said Maria.
"Kids and adults should talk to those kids who are afraid
and help them overcome their fears," said Juan.
"If we don't talk to each other,
we'll live all our lives with that pain."

"We came closer together and grew, and we knew that even if
something so terrible as this could happen, we could pull together
and pull the pieces together," said Courtney.

Little by little, the children learned
that healing takes patience and time.
They discovered new ways to spend their days
as faith and hope began to fill hearts
that once held sadness and pain.

"I don't know why," said Emili,
"but it helped to write it down on paper...to see it.
I have a journal for writing things down."
"You can draw pictures," said William.
"You can try to set some goals for yourself
so you can work toward something
instead of spending all your time thinking about a bomb,"
said Dillon. "Something else that helped me
is that I got two new dogs
and I spend a lot of time playing with them."
"If my friends can't get a dog," said Leigh,
"they can always come over to my house
and play with my dog."
"We need to stick together through bad times," said Abby.

"It's better if we help each other and share," said Lilia.

As the fear faded
and the hurt healed,
shock and loss started to disappear.
Routines returned to normal,
life took on new meaning,
and the world began to feel safe again.

"It took weeks for me to feel better,"
said Jaclyn.
"We felt bad for months," said Joshua.

"It took a long time for me," said Adam.
"It helped me feel better when I helped
other people."

As if watching a picture come slowly into focus,
the children began to understand that
pain makes us value what we lost,
and loss makes us treasure what we have.

"This has made me appreciate my family more,"
said Cicely.
"You never know when something's going to happen,"
said Alecia.
"Every day is a different day," said Argelia.
"And I think you should appreciate every day
like it was the last day of your life."
"If your mom's mad at you, apologize that day,"
said Aimee Ann. "There may not be a tomorrow."
"When Forrest Gump was in Vietnam," said Cicely,
"he said, 'If I would have known this was the last time
I'd see my best good friend Bubba, I would have said
something different.'"

"Never take for granted what you have," said Stephanie.

After the bomb,
after the shock and sadness,
after the anger and grief,
the children learned
that the road to recovery is long and bumpy
and that some wounds never truly heal.
They also learned
that even when their world has changed forever,
they can still make it a better place
by filling the lives around them
with goodness and kindness and love.

*"Helping the families and trying to get them to recuperate
made us feel better," said Courtney.
"It made us feel like it was all coming to a close."*

"This will stay in my heart forever," said Aimee Ann.

*"Things get better," said Cicely, "even if you do have
that place in your heart where it still hurts."*

AFTER

Four days after the bombing, the president and Hillary Rodham Clinton flew to Oklahoma City for a memorial service that helped to heal a grieving nation.

Throughout the long, painful recovery period, Governor Frank Keating and his wife, Cathy Keating, and Lt. Governor Mary Fallin, along with Mayor Ron Norick and his wife, Carolyn Norick, visited the bomb site every day. They talked to weary rescue workers, comforted mourning families, sat with people waiting to find out about their loved ones, assisted in the rescue efforts, and helped out in any way they could.

In the beginning, when news of the bombing was broadcast across the nation, hundreds of disaster experts and charity workers, pastors and engineers, counselors and nurses and law-enforcement officials, fire fighters and rescue teams and search dogs, came from all over the United States to help.

Over 120,000 free meals for the rescue workers and other volunteers were provided by the Oklahoma Restaurant Association. The Salvation Army donated another hundred thousand meals and drinks.

The Boy Scouts of America helped in the rescue and clean-up operations, and the Camp Fire Boys and Girls provided day camp for children who had immediate family members killed or injured in the blast.

Seven hundred fifty to one thousand rescue workers dug through the rubble to find survivors in the Murrah building. They came from Oklahoma, Arizona, California, Florida, Maryland, New York, Virginia, and Washington.

Twenty-four dog-and-man teams participated in the search-and-rescue efforts.

According to the Oklahoma Blood Institute, Oklahomans donate blood at twice the national average. That was the only reason there was enough blood immediately on hand to supply hospitals during the first few hours of the crisis. Three days later, over seven thousand additional pints had been donated, more than enough to provide for the needs of most of the state for several weeks. Hundreds of offers of even more blood came from throughout the country and around the world, demonstrating the care and concern of people everywhere.

Oklahoma City's main library, which was devastated by the bomb, received donations of $22,115 and 274 books.

Over three thousand members of the FBI worked on the case, and over $10 million has been spent to bring the criminals to justice.

Over $20 million has been donated to help the people affected by the bombing rebuild their lives.

Even now, the recovery continues. And even now, people continue to help one another.

The following children generously participated in the writing of this book.

Connie Aguirre

Erika Aguirre

Michael Aguirre

Chad Ashley

Tiara Clytus

Brad Collier

Jamie Conway

John Conway

Ramsey Conway

Jenna DeHekker

Matt DeHekker

Rachel Flesher

Ryan Flesher

Jack Funk

William Funk

Argelia Garcia

Juan Luis Garcia

Leticia Garcia

Lilia Garcia

Maria Garcia

Stephanie Gilmore

Emili Gragg

Leigh Hefner

Virginia Hefner

Abby Harris

Bonny Harris

Dillon Helm

Gracie Helm

Christina Kueteman

Austin Lockard

Elizabeth Lockard

Todd Lockard

Deana Nelson

Aleah Parker

Ashley Parker

Adam Patten

Courtney Patten

Addi Schnebel

Bailey Schnebel

Macey Stapleton

Melissa Tackett

Alecia R. Thomas

Jaclyn Thompson

Joshua Thompson

Aimee Ann Vanek

Brendon Williams

Darbi Williams

Cicely Williams

Julie Elaine Wolf

Eleanor Zachery

With heartfelt gratitude to the following consultants, whose wisdom, insight, and understanding made this a better book:
Mary Ann Coates, L.C.S.W., B.C.D., Anne Early, L.C.S.W., A.C.S.W.,
The Right Reverend C. Shannon Mallory.
And with thanks to those others who contributed their time
and effort to help make this book a reality:
Audrey Baker, M.Ed., Mary Beth Berney, Carol Blank, Lee Bollinger, The Rev. Susan Colley,
Representative Odilia Dank, Kay Hardwick Davidson, William Davidson, Patricia De Moraes,
Ruby Evans, Lisa Ransom Flesher, Seyann Hefner, Ginny Gill Jacobs, John Koons, Kay Rhodes,
Martha Rogers, The Rev. Melvin E. Truiett, Sr., Janet Zarem, Megan Zwoyer.
And a special thank-you to Andrea Brown, agent extraordinaire.